D0629764

WORDS
THAT SHINE BOTH WAYS

Other books by Richard Moss:

The I That is We
How Shall I Live
The Black Butterfly
The Second Miracle

WORDS
THAT SHINE BOTH WAYS

REFLECTIONS THAT RECONNECT US
TO OUR TRUE NATURE

RICHARD MOSS, M.D.

Compiled and Introduced
by Gill Goater

Enneas Publications
OAKHURST, CALIFORNIA

First published in 1998 by Enneas Publications
Oakhurst, California

For further information contact:
Enneas Publications
P.O. Box 2147
Oakhurst, California 93644

Packaged by The Book Laboratory, USA
Illustrations © Moon*runner* Design, U.K
Design & typesetting by Moon*runner* Design, U.K.
Edited and compiled by Gill Goater
Printed in the United States of America

Library of Congress Catalogue in Publication Data

Moss, Richard M., 1947-
    Words That Shine Both Ways / by Richard Moss
    p.   cm.
ISBN 0-9659820-0-9
1. Philosophy.   2. Spirituality.   I. Title

Library of Congress Catalog Card Number: 97-77336

Contents

Author's Preface

WHEN GILL GOATER, A FRIEND AND LONG-TIME STUDENT OF my work, approached me with the idea of creating a book of quotes that she had culled from my talks given at various seminars over the years, I was pleased but a little doubtful. The spoken word often does not migrate easily into written form, and that has been particularly true for me. Perhaps this is because, aside from poetry, our brains are conditioned to expect a more linear organization of ideas in written material. When I am teaching, I let go into a relationship with a deeper awareness. This relationship is at once within me and with the individuals who are offering me their attention. The words emerge spontaneously and my experience is that they are riding on a current of energy or presence. They flow forth organizing themselves in unexpected ways that can be quite insightful and often trigger deeply felt spaces in the listeners and in me as well. Indeed, these are words that shine both ways, in that they illumine us into a deeper relationship to ourselves which simultaneously becomes a fresh perception of that which is universal.

I am delighted and moved by the sensitivity and intelligence with which Gill has managed to maintain the feeling, insight and ambiguity of these extemporaneously spoken thoughts. Trusting her own response, she has selected quotes that have resonated in her and has grouped them according to a general theme applicable to my teaching. Perhaps most importantly, she has rendered them in a visual form that allows our poetic awareness the space to receive them. I trust the reader will be enriched by her effort. At the suggestion of several people who read the first manuscript, I have provided additional threads of teaching in counterpoint to certain of the quotes. These appear at the bottom of the page in a different print font. My intention was to further ground the meaning suggested in the quotes. I am very grateful to Gill for creating this opportunity to invite you into a relationship with me, or at least with the state of being that has led me to express these words.

In service to Life with you,

Richard Moss

Foreword

I AM DRIVING TOWARDS MY FIRST MEETING with Richard Moss and the birthplace of this book. It is very hot in the mini bus and the landscape is unfamiliar—ochre and yellow and dull green, a sagebrush plain arid beyond my imagining. A dirt road snakes through huge rocks—a road so narrow at times that the sides of the vehicle I am traveling in barely scrape by. I watch the dust swirl and glitter in the dry brightness; and when it settles the clarity in the air draws me upwards through the burning blue into immensity without end.

The vehicle funnels through a narrowing of the road and emerges into a tiny valley encircled by ancient boulders, heaped like fallen gods. I step out of the bus and my body quivers. I am dazed with the shock of such unanticipated beauty. I feel silky grass tickling my bare feet for I have kicked off my sandals—one does not go shod in Paradise. The air smells of moisture and ripeness and I see gnarled fig trees laden with fruit and peach and almond trees and grapes heavy on the vine. Richard's conferences transport one out of one's familiar reality and already the landscape has begun this work.

I've been to many conferences with Richard Moss since

that day in 1989, both as participant and associate, though never again at Hidden Valley. Each time is a different experience. I've wondered about that and decided that I bring a different me each time; a me that reflects the ongoing process of change, of emotional and spiritual maturing that these experiential conferences generate. Often something Richard has said will take up lodgings in my heart and work a subtle alteration throughout the year, like yeast in dough.

This book is a collection of words Richard Moss has spoken over the years, during conferences or lectures. I have simply organized them into lines and spaces that reflect the intonations of the spoken word. They are grouped together under themes which are central to Richard's work. I have preceded each section with a brief explanation to give you a context for a deeper understanding.

The quotes have a life of their own. You may find they have the power to shift your perspective and to bring you to a new awareness. It is like planting seeds that grow in the soul. There is an inductiveness in many of them which works beyond the level of the rational mind. They can touch and awaken the deep vein of mysticism in the human psyche, communicating meaning even where the intellect cannot follow. Read them like poetry, where the literal meaning is supplemented by many layers and levels and textures, unspoken intuitions and glimpses of essence.

You'll notice in the quotes that God is mentioned frequently. It was hard work leaping that barrier after turning away from the Church in disappointment in my early twenties. What kind of a man is this who talks so freely about God and what is his frame of reference? Is God simply an evocative word for soul, for the intelligence that creates this complex web of interconnectedness in which we live? We've been battered by dogma, man-made ideas on the nature of God. What happens when we remove the attempt to define God and intuit, if we are truthful, our real ignorance of what God is? What happens when the word God simply suggests to us—mystery? Or a oneness with all of life or the deeper intelligence of the universe or the sacred act of attention or the holiness of the breath? What happens when we remove the knowing around the word God?

I believe the words in this book are our possible future, beckoning us towards a path we can all travel if we are honest and humble enough to admit that there is no map for this territory called being. Dare we embrace the mystery of ourselves and our relationship to each other and to existence; do we hear the call to awakening that is resounding through the web of consciousness that links us? Life has no certainty and acknowledging its mystery, beauty and pain can bring us to our knees in simple wonder. Are we willing to surrender to what is more than genetically encoded in us, to embrace these intimations of our vast potential and limitless possibility?

These words have seeded states of great joy in me and have been a spark of inner brilliance in some very dark times too, times when I had lost all delight in being alive. They have expanded me and comforted me, excited me and humbled me, made me laugh and cry and exult in the beauty and the transcendent brilliance of human possibility. I hope you get as much from reading this book as I have in putting it together.

I've been using these quotes for several years, copying them out for myself or to give to friends. It has been a wonderful way of sharing what moves in me when I cannot find my own words to express it and I enjoy seeing the poems touch the hearts of others. Often I pin a quote on my refrigerator or by the side of my bed watching how they change my energy. Sometimes I choose one at random and trust that it has meaning for me in that moment. It has become a pathway for my own intuition and a good way to prepare myself for meditation.

I hope the words in this book will switch on a light to shine within you, both as a beacon to guide you and as a source of inspiration to lead you in faith and hope through this challenging time.

With love

Gill Goater

Meditation

T HE OPENING OF THE HEART—our ability to live from our authentic nature—is the core of Richard Moss' teaching. An open heart presumes a deep meditative awareness, a radical intuition of self, of *that-which-precedes-thought*. Otherwise we are constantly at the mercy of our thoughts, happy when they are positive and miserable when they are negative.

There are many different practices for approaching the state known as meditation. Generally, all involve stabilizing awareness by employing some form of focused attention. For example, we can repeat a mantra: a phrase or sound such as "Alleluia" or "Yes". Other forms utilize awareness of breath with or without special consideration of posture.

Richard Moss often refers to the awareness of breath or mantra as analogous to a conductor's baton. It provides a background against which we begin to simply witness the activity of our minds. In so doing we gradually become present to the space of awareness itself. In these quotes the heart of meditation is revealed beyond allegiance to any specific technique.

Meditation is laughing at yourself.
  I know probably no one's ever said
  that's what meditation is.

For twenty minutes or so
  hopefully every day
  or for moments throughout the day
  you learn to just observe mind.

You tether the mind, softly anchoring
  its attention, in some way.

By tethering the mind
  it becomes possible to notice
  everything else you do with the mind.

Smiling softly at how clever
  the mind is at trapping you
  in ideas, images, fears
  and plans...ceaselessly.

Anything but being simply present,
  simply you, simply free
  now.

Laughing, not taking our minds and therefore ourselves so seriously, is to discover space, to discover God.

S<small>AY</small> we tether the mind
   by silently repeating the word "yes"

It's an approximate translation of the word "om"
   Om means "yes to life, yes to what is".

What arises out of this practice
   is just a witness, just an observer.

Now I'm happy
   now I'm unhappy
   now I feel pain
   now I'm blissful.

When finally we have tethered the mind
   we begin to intuit what's prior to mind.

Some meditation follows the breath
becoming very receptive
to whatever arises in consciousness
being centered in the body
aware of the breath and using it
as an anchor point for the attention.

One of the images is the image of a river
and down the river floats a thought
and it floats by, you observe it
and then it floats out of sight.

Or a cloudless sky
and then comes a sensation
or a feeling, or a memory pattern
and it's a cloud
and you learn to observe it
and you learn to laugh at yourself.

You learn to laugh at
any thought process that comes up.

It doesn't matter if it's of God or popcorn
or the desire to feel good
or the desire for peace of mind.

And finally we understand
that anything we can laugh at
no longer has hooks into our soul.

I GET into this meditation
and all of a sudden I fall asleep
and I'm gone.

What is that?

That's meditation
that split second released from all technique
before you fall asleep
or space out.

DURING meditation,
   if the attention wanders
   you split—off into thinking, memories, plans
   and the energy level drops.

The paradox is
   that the more you relax
   the more the danger
   that the mind will wander aimlessly
   and you'll space out.

Simultaneously
   the more you relax
   the greater the likelihood
   of simply falling into attention
   falling into a simple attention.

That is the fundamental
   paradox of meditation.

It's to be completely relaxed
   yet fully present.

*Meditation isn't a stress reduction technique.
It's a way of recognizing the ego and the process of seeing
ego naturally relaxes its hold over awareness.*

WHEN we come home to ourselves
the breath pumps bliss in a great space
of silent being.

Hearing these words the ego says
  "I want this. I have to do a lot of work
  before I can come home.
  I have to be worthy."

But the place that really nourishes us
  receives us in some mysterious way
  and doesn't really care
  what we've done
  or who we think we are
  or what we imagine we need to do.

🌿   *Again and again our egos seduce us into the
search, into striving. The ego tells us we cannot be sufficient
as we are. It demands we contract in doubt, in sorrow, in
fear. Then it is secure once again.*

DON'T go into meditation thinking
how powerful it can be
how vast it can be.

Go into it realizing your own innate frailty.

There's something incredibly resilient
about the human psyche,
but if you've ever come close
to feeling it broken loose
from its moorings
in subject-object consciousness,
if you've ever felt the terror
of that opening upon infinity
the extraordinary frailty
of the human consciousness
the frailty of the soul
as it looks out on infinity...

If you've felt that then you know humility.

🔥 *Ultimately, meditation can bring us to the abyss where self and other collapses into I AM THAT I AM. For the sovereign ego this sometimes feels like annihilation. But it really is just humiliation, humiliation of our ego-centric point of view, so that the ego becomes the servant of awareness and not the determiner of our sense of self.*

I<small>T</small>'s territory that nobody, no mind
really grasps or understands.

You can't go into meditation
assuming you'll expand, get calm,
become enlightened, that everything
will be just fine.

You can't go into
any deep energetic communion with that
self-serving ambition.

Sitting in meditation, even the subtle quality of expectancy can be a form of contraction, a dynamic of the ego.

ONE of the enormous jumps in meditation
is to become aware
of who wants to meditate
and who doesn't want to meditate.

Because behind the one who does or doesn't
is what the Buddhists refer to as desire body.

You can find desire body everywhere

And to be able to observe desire body
not push it away or engage it or energize it
is the beginning of freedom.

MEDITATION holds the possibility

of collapsing the separation

between thinking and being,

between me and you

between me and God.

MEDITATION is the art of intimacy with oneself.

Intimacy with the agitation and the stillness of mind.

Intimacy with how awareness collapses into moods,
   into pain and discomfort, into reminiscing, into
   plans and creates the continuous series of me(s)
   — that endlessly sustain our egos.

> Me who loves
> Me who fears
> Me who strives
> Me who capitulates
> despairs, exults, dies
> Me(s) to fix

Intimate with all this and not to judge,
   just to see, to feel
   the presence of awareness.

THE heart of meditation is allowing.

The presence of awareness
   does not lose itself in all the shapes
   we call ourselves.

It is no more or less in our peace
   or our heartache.

But how to see
   to simply be aware
   that anything we experience
   we are already larger than.

Decide to be fully present

Don't become an accomplice
  to any thought, any desire.

See how everything we do or want
  is a way of avoiding relationship

Now

Attention

W HAT IS ATTENTION in the sense that it is used in the following quotations?

Every second of every day, our internal and external environments batter us with thousands of stimuli—ideas, feelings, images, sounds, body sensations and so on. To survive this onslaught on our consciousness, we have to filter out most of the input. Over the years as our egos are developing, we become highly selective in what we allow into our awareness. We form habits.

We have a choice of what we will notice from moment to moment and this greatly affects the quality of our lives.

If what we choose to focus on helps us to grow into emotional and spiritual maturity, develop intimate relationships with ourselves and others, then the way we use our attention enhances our aliveness.

If we habitually split from our feelings or if we are too identified with our mind chatter to be present to what is really happening, then we deaden ourselves. We become less connected, less capable of intimacy, less likely to experience moments of radical aliveness which is our human potential.

For example, suppose that when I'm angry or upset, my attention is on what is going through my mind. Perhaps I think about how this always happens to me or how unfair life is or how dare he yell at me and so on. That is one choice. We are all familiar with that kind of thinking. It fuels the anger.

What would happen if instead, I acknowledged I was feeling angry and directed my attention to my breath and to the sensation of anger in my body, noticing, watching, holding sensation and breath within my awareness? What happens to the fires of anger then? Perhaps I will see how minute by minute my internal scenery changes. Maybe I will intuit into what my body could do to express the energy held within its boundaries. Perhaps it will shift into something else. Perhaps I will re-establish the connection I lost when I was a child and anger was simply a body experience that flowed through me into authentic expression. There are so many possibilities.

The heart of all spiritual training everywhere is attention. This section explores its many facets, challenging us to discover and examine the patterns in our own lives.

ATTENTION is the single
most important resource
that human beings
have

and it's so obvious
that it's one of our resources
that we're never even aware
we have it.

 Attention isn't what we hear or see, it is the
capacity to listen, to perceive.

ATTENTION is energy
and anything that holds you present
builds energy.

If people are really present
the whole vibration in the room
thickens and refines.

It's like sitting in a force field.

 *No athlete performs at their peak if their minds
are in the past or future.*

ALL spiritual training

the very heart of it

is developing attention,

because to have attention

is to have presence.

I AM so deeply trusting
  of what happens to us
  when we start to really listen
  to what life is asking

for in the very act of listening
  we start to become available
  to what we truly need.

Our egos want to control and direct our experience and this weakens us because unknowingly we've become the victims of fear.

IF you're truly present
  to a deeper level of yourself

if you're really listening
  within your own bodymind

you're exquisitely responsive
  to what appears outside.

Some people's *I amness* is strong
  in a context that's familiar
and they lose it in another context.

Real *I amness*
  migrates beautifully

  anywhere.

🌱   *We confuse our natural being, our I amness
with our persona, our personal identity. Then we fit or don't
fit as situations change.*

SPONTANEOUS creativity

is a universal attitude

of attention.

Attention isn't passive. It is a dynamic relationship that aligns us with the natural unfolding of life moment by moment.

THE vast majority of time our speech
comes from the past
or is about the future.

God's not speaking.

The creator's not speaking.

The created is speaking
in an endless loop of self absorption.

The direct connection
to that which is life is dead.

🌿   *In the West we speak of body, mind and spirit.
But in certain Eastern traditions the triad is body, mind and
voice. For spirit is what lives us as we express ourselves out of
the immediacy of the present.*

THE laying on of hands
  is about the mystery of attention
  but it becomes a *healing* ritual
  and the real mystery is lost.

Sacred Meditation, Reiki, Aura Balancing -
  they're fundamentally
  exercises in subtle attention
  but they get co-opted
  by the ego
  and into the structure
  of spiritual healing and energy therapy and so on.

Which is why we experience so much
  and learn so little.

🌿   *When we no longer have to trick ourselves with*
"special" situations to shift our attention toward the Infinite,
then we are already always healers, always showering a
radiance of presence. Nothing special.

ENLIGHTENMENT is faith.

Faith usually means
    that you can take a series of beliefs
    and you can hold onto them
    and that's your faith.

That's all about fear.

What real faith is,
    that this entity, this organism,
    in the midst of intense feeling
    stays.

All our work is about that
    not how to get away
    but how to stay.

THE greatest gift we give each other
is the quality of our attention.

Where is Mother Theresa's attention
when she picks up a starving child?

It's in the Christ

That she sees
within her
and within the child

It's in the infinity
the unending mystery.

Yes.

THE way I like to think about the Sabbath
is that we kind of screwed it up
remembering God on the one day.
What if we said one seventh of our attention
at any given moment
is towards infinity
is towards unboundedness
is towards God?
One seventh of my attention.
Just enough to make me know
no matter how much
I like or dislike you
no matter how frozen I am
in my judgments of you
one seventh of me is infinitely unfrozen
and you are slowly going to shape-change before
my eyes and in my heart.
Six sevenths of me grasps you
in a particular way
and six sevenths of you grasps me.
But one seventh of both of us
is reaching out
and shape changing our world
                    moment
                    by moment
                    by moment
                    not forgetting God.

Mystery

THIS SECTION ON MYSTERY embraces all that we cannot know about ourselves and the nature of our universe and God. Moment by moment we are invited to enter into a relationship with mystery, to stand at this edge of unknowing in ourselves. A proper relationship may be to approach mystery as a sacred vessel to carry us closer to its heart and our own. In this way we may live in the knowledge of that which is unnameable.

Rest in mystery
for it is the cradle
of the divine
in each of us.

Rest in mystery
for it is the crucible
wherein our gold
is given birth.

Embrace unknowing
for it is the unraveler
of the thread
that holds together
our mistaken certainty.

Embrace unknowing
for it is the sea
that binds the raindrop
in great tides of mystery.

Embrace unknowing
for it is the weaver
whose silken web
enfolds us in eternity.

A poem by *Gill Goater*

Some of us have the intuition
  of the divine
  directly
  so we're not especially drawn
  to any kind of teaching or teacher.

The immediacy of the divine is present.

Some of us are drawn
  to teachings and teachers
  to the degree
  that we accept their ability
  to perceive or intuit mystery
  and interpret it for us.

The universe is so generous
  that it will give us mystery
  in any way we are capable of seeing it.

Where is the transformational journey going now?

There'll always be those souls
    who set aside ordinary life
    in order to rise up to God.

And there'll always be those souls
    who are totally immersed in ordinary life
    and don't give a thought to God.

But the next evolutionary step
    is in those who continue
    to feel God in everything
    and embrace this ordinary life.

They are in a terribly difficult tension.

❧   *This tension leads to intellectual subtlety, to
greater emotional depth and compassion, to a fuller expression
of our humanness. The growing wholeness of our humanity
is our growing divinity.*

Wᴴᴬᵀ happens in the hearts
of the great souls
is that they enter into territory
which is beyond their ability to relate to
and either they're destroyed by it
or their hearts get big enough
to contain that experience
and if they return
the boundaries of possibility
have been enlarged
for everyone.

Could this be happening to you now?
But you call it divorce, or illness, or failure, or depression.

Iꜰ at the time of death
we can live into our experience
utterly and completely
it's possible
that the energy
that shines forth from us then
may be the greatest service
we've ever been able to give to life.

It may shine out
as the transforming elixir
for all of life, everywhere.

 This is also the essence of the Tibetan teaching about the bardo stages at death. For a brief while we become a doorway connecting the finite and the infinite, a great heart in which everything is reconciled. And this is also what happens during realization when the ego is fully submitted to the larger reality.

THE experience of being at the edge

of encountering death

is really a mystical initiation.

What is it

that allows me

to touch my own experience

in faith?

🔥   *Death is the ultimate humiliation to our egos.*
Suddenly we realize that we are much more than we ever
allowed. Faith, itself is a great mystery; relationship and
connection without rational explanation.

To love the Lord thy God
with all thy heart and soul and mind
is an amazing thing.

That relationship…
it expands the room
the walls fall away.

You say, "I feel frustrated
because it's not happening
the way I want it to", or
"I don't understand
what's happening now…"

But when you add that ineffable quality
which is the first commandment
you realize it's crazy
to try to understand your life
because life is mystery
forever dark to the mind.

But what is dark to the mind
is, in faith, radiant to the heart.

THE more we live deeply into life
the more we turn to God.

And the more we turn to God
the more we live deeply into life.

When we turn towards mystery

        mystery
        parades through our lives.

N<small>OBODY</small>
comes to peace of mind
except through incredible struggle
because no one
would rest in God
save that they had
tried to have life on their terms and failed
in every imaginable way.

Faith emerges
out of how much
we've tried and failed.

 *Faith is not a technique for protection from suffering. It is a relationship to Mystery that we can be brought to in our suffering.*

IT takes tremendous maturity
to meet life
to really meet life
to meet all of life
and not to make ourselves wrong
in the suffering.

And that's what makes us radiant.

GOD got lost
and keeps getting lost
and therefore it's difficult
to apprehend the Mystery.

What we do is
   we change God into an object
   which is why we can march
   in the name of this God
   against those who march
   in the name of another God.

Ego has once again
   co-opted Mystery.

*God is never reducible to any concept. When
God is an idea, no matter how subtle, this is idolatry.
God is always "lost" when we imagine we can imagine God.*

THE ego always asks how
and makes it a weapon
against aliveness
which isn't to say
we should never have a how.

In the finite world how is crucial.

There is a way
  to make a good soufflé.

There is a way
  to solve a mathematical problem.

In the finite world how is relevant.

But the minute you walk into
  the cathedral of yourself
  you're in the infinite.

There isn't any how in the infinite.

❦   *Jesus said this simply, "Give unto Caesar what
is Caesar's and give unto God what is God's."*

WHAT we've learned
what has been hard won
through struggle
our children learn more easily
just by being in the great web
of connectedness
the great web of relationship.

The things that we did
that took us a whole lifetime to find
someone else has straight away.

They have it instantly
they don't even know why they have it.

The reason is that there's no such thing
as an individual.

Not in an ultimate sense.

*If we will let ourselves get quiet enough and
accept our own experience, we can each know what Jesus
knew, what Buddha knew, and we ourselves can bring forth
new possibility for everyone else.*

THERE'S no certainty.

If you really look closely at life
   you'll see that there's no certainty.

We've used enormous amounts of energy
   to create predictability
   and we pay for it with depression
   we pay for it with cancer
   we pay for it with chemicals
   and food additives and everything else
   to make sure that what we want
   is there when we want it.

And then that's not what
   we really want.

*When will we finally accept that the only
possible relationship to life's uncertainty is faith?*

WE'VE tried to be absorbed in God
and pushed away the world
and that was a mistake.

And we've been
   so absorbed in the world
   that we've pushed away God
   and that's been a mistake.

And holding the two
   at whatever level we can
   that's really what the journey is.

As the faith deepens
   every time I've had to experience
   something difficult in my life
   and I've said, "O.K. I'm about to die."

I've not died and
   greater beauty has grown.

Jesus said, "Where two or three
   are gathered together
   in my name
   there shall I be
   in the midst of them."

And it will be like a living presence,
   a gentle current
   a softening in your heart
   easefulness
   a subtle, quiet happiness.

But you have to put your bags down
   and feel it.

*So what are these bags? Our need for security,
our need to be in control, our need for approval, our need
for understanding. Ramana Maharshi used the image that
we are traveling on a train. "Why then", he asked, "won't
we put our baggage down?"*

If we can come through a number of years
of deep exploration
and get out of the mode
of fixing ourselves up
or acquiring something
and drop into something
that is much more fundamental
greater and greater self revelation
greater and greater revelation
of our own beingness...

That magnetizes and generates
the capacity for exploration
anywhere we go.

And that
we can stand on forever.

There is no end to the ego's strategies to avoid discomfort, to avoid seeing itself. To live this way is to build your house on sand.

Iт's really important
  for us to be humbled

Humbled in a way
  that comes from
  being awed

Humbling that comes from
  the wonderment
  of how rich we each are

To look at a soul
  and feel the enormous majesty
  the mystery of another human being

To see the divine shine through
  another human being.

Unconditional Love

W<small>E USE THE WORD LOVE</small> to express many ways of relating to people, things and ideas. We talk about loving people and horses and skiing and justice and truth and chocolate.

And they all represent a different kind of relationship.

For most of us unconditional love is less ambiguous. It expresses a way of loving ourselves or another person without condition. Total acceptance of another human being in all they do, say, think or feel.

Unconditional love according to Richard is a vast and mysterious potential within us; it is an unconditional relationship to the whole of existence.

Mechtild de Magdeburg, a medieval mystic, said the same thing when she asked, "*How shall I live?*" and was answered "*Live welcoming to all.*" This was a blueprint for loving unconditionally.

When Richard personifies Existence I can sense more easily the complex and paradoxical nature of unconditional love.

Existence is everything; both the part and the whole, inclusive and accepting of all things—cockroaches, eagles, human beings, death, famine, music, war.

Existence impersonally knows both future and past: knows the perfect rightness of every second. Existence accepts all, without attachment, with such a broad sweep of vision that its parts—including us, seem almost inconsequential.

The one imperative of Existence is to bring the conscious part of itself, which includes human beings, to a realization of its preexisting wholeness. And what matters to us does not appear of consequence to Existence in its vast movement towards self-awareness.

An unconditional acceptance of each moment may be the closest that we human beings can come to the unconditional lovingness of existence, a saying yes to life, a saying yes to that which continually unfolds around and within us.

UNCONDITIONAL love looks at you
and looks at the walls
the sky, the trees
and everything else the same.

Unconditional love, loves you
but it loves everyone else identically.

It's not something we do.

It's what already is.

And it can't be lived by us.

It lives through us.

WE don't win love.
We come to a space
in which love happens of itself.

🌿 *Our egos imagine that love is our reward for its
striving to be good, to succeed…but love gifts us when our
urge, our effort, our striving relaxes.*

Wʜᴀᴛ unconditional love
looks like to me
for our age
and our time
is not finding
a belief or process
that will make you happy,
but having the strength
and courage to stay present
for whatever you experience
       not as a victim,
       not righteous in it,
       not as an evangelist
for some idea, some technique, some faith,
       but just to stay present.

IT's the thing you can't say 'Yes' to

that is your door to the Universe.

 *When we say 'No' in a way that closes us to life, love pushes against this resistance and we suffer until we can open.*

TRYING to force ourselves open

to feel something positive

that isn't here of itself

is a cruelty.

 The art is learning to allow what we really feel.

JUST CARE.

You can't save your life
  so care.

You can't get conscious
  in the hope that it will keep you
  from getting a disease
  so care.

You can't be assured
  that awakening won't make you crazy
  so just care.

In the end
  when all of your strategies for salvation
  don't work
  will you be able to stop
  in the existential nakedness of yourself
  wounded beyond knowing,
  naked, absolutely naked
  and pick yourself up
  and access your will to be

Nothing...but caring?

As our acceptance deepens, compassion awakens.

I**F** you really know that you're loved
that the Universe is loving
then you can walk
through incredibly dark places
where other people can't walk
where they are crushed by the abyss.

Authentic faith always stands side by side with the abyss.

WHEN the tremendous presence
of unconditional love
flames within you,
you are not saying
"This is love."

You are not saying
    anything at all.

To talk about this presence later
    is already a distortion.

Unconditional love
    is quite beyond words.

When it is there
    you are not.

Healing

WE PROBABLY UNDERSTAND the concept of healing better now in the twentieth century than at any other time in recorded history—and we barely understand it at all.

Richard left the practice of conventional medicine many years ago but his work continues to be about medicine—medicine for the soul and the psyche as well as the body. It is about healing the woundedness within us, healing of that which separates us from experiencing our own wholeness, preventing us from realizing our full physical, emotional and spiritual flowering. Despite the breadth of modern medical knowledge and technology, ease and disease retain an element of mystery that is beyond our efforts to quantify, explain and control. Some of the quotations suggest new ways to relate to illness, ways that acknowledge the workings of a deep collective intelligence. We may find ourselves in a disease process not because we are doing something wrong but because that may be the very best effort of existence to bring us to wholeness.

There are valuable insights in these quotations for self healing and for those who work as healers.

WHEN we are functioning well
we may not be healthy.

When we are functioning poorly
we may not be unhealthy.

We are most radiant
when we can't tell
whether we're functioning
well or not.

   I believe that often we function well and we
feel good because the ego is too well defended. It succeeds in
repressing so much life force that while we don't suffer, this
repressed energy eventually becomes cancer and other diseases.
When we are more open, this deeper life force demands that
we feel and that we grow. This can be very uncomfortable
and we can seem to ourselves dysfunctional, but from the
point of view of life's greater intelligence this may be healthy.

Nobody ever heals themselves
   because they're told
   they have a brain tumor.

They heal themselves because
   they enter their own experience
   profoundly and originally

In the present.

You can't go back
   and fall into your past
   to heal yourself.

You have to come
   totally into the present.

🌿   *It is our direct intimacy with ourselves, not the labels we use about ourselves that brings forth the energy for healing.*

THE secret
of self healing
is to find
that one part of you
that can be truly creative
and authentic
then follow that
with tremendous intensity
and the kind of will
that took
a Christ
into forty days
and forty nights
in the desert.

I DON'T know what to do with despair.
And either I'm whole in that or I'm not.
Nobody has ever known what to do with despair.
The next time you feel despair
  and you don't know what you're going to do
  and it's unacceptable to be paralyzed in that
  just start jogging up a steep hill,
  know that you won't quit till the top
  and pretty soon there's no despair.
How in the world could you be wrestling your
  body up a steep hill, jogging, burning your lungs out
  perhaps getting ready to have a coronary,
  and still be despairing?
The energy gets transferred to something else.
Or sing about it.
Get up and sing about it
Sing it out.
"I feel like shit and I don't know
  what the hell I'm doing
  and nothing's working right."
Just sing it louder and louder
  because when you do
  life force is being celebrated.

🕭   *Life energy not used tends to become morbid.*
No mood exists in itself. It is always an expression of a
pattern of containing energy. Change the pattern—laugh,
curse, sing, paint, dance—and the energy releases. Then
spontaneously, we naturally tend to reorganize in wholeness.

I CAN try to keep manipulating
my consciousness, my self awareness
so I feel good.

Or I can take the risk
of feeling this agony of unknowing
this nakedness before existence.
I can try to let my heart open
where I don't know how to be.

And that's evolution.
That's growth.

Every time in my life I have sat in pain
and stopped protecting myself from it
something has come and taken me
into a nectar of exquisite clarity.

*First we must learn to release morbid patterns.
But eventually acceptance is the greatest elixir.*

At a time when I didn't know if I had the
capacity to balance the forces that I was dealing
with in this life,

I realized that serious disease might be one
possible response or adaptation.

And I knew if my body actually developed a disease,
a cancer or whatever,
it would be out of the very best
effort of existence
to find a way to integrate the energy.

I wouldn't be a failure. Wholeness would only
choose that path if it were the best path it could
find given the circumstances of who I was.

 We are not victims unless we choose to be.

THE question is
    can we fix ourselves with our egos?

And my answer to that is no
    I don't believe we can.

That doesn't go over well
    with the people who feel that
    with our rational minds
    we can solve all problems
    including problems of the soul.

I think we have to reach a point
    where we cannot grow any longer
    through any act of our own ego.

And that's what I call
    the wound the ego cannot heal.

LIFE finally presents us face on
    with the wound the ego cannot heal.

And as long as we keep trying
    to heal it with our egos
    there's no end to the misery.

There isn't any place to reach
    yet we try and try and try.

Our separation fear, the emptiness
    we abhor is our distance from our real self.

Into this void we project
    the notion of a path,
    the folly of endless seeking.

🌿   *What is the wound the ego cannot heal? It
cannot heal the sense of separateness that it, itself, is the root
of. It cannot heal aloneness. It cannot heal its own original
terror of non-existence.*

WE HAVE to overcome
the wound of the ego
the wound the ego is

and the paradox of that
is that we overcome it
by reaching a place
where we're so terribly wounded
that the ego cannot heal it.

No ego can heal it.
No intellect can heal it.
Only faith heals it
and faith is abundant.

Spirit heals it
and spirit is limitless.

🌿 *Naïve faith tries to give over our suffering to God before we have truly entered fully into it. Not suffering for suffering's sake, but led by our wounds to the depths of our humanness. This fear of suffering is where much religion and New Age spirituality acts in the service of denial. It is the redemptive power of conscious suffering that leads to mature faith.*

Can you be injured
by the energy of another?

No, never by their energy.

You are only injured by how you
react to them in your own
consciousness.

THE organism itself is so profoundly repressed
by what we call adulthood.

So profoundly repressed that sometimes only
violence will get it loosened up.

The violence of divorce
The violence of disease
The violence of drugs
The violence of intense ceremonies

Sometimes we need these things.

But we have to be honest.
They're violent.
Hyperventilation for several hours is violent.
Long meditation retreats are violent.

Sometimes
we're so tremendously repressed
that violence is what is called for.

I've come to the conclusion
  that what I do in my work
  could happen anywhere
  if only we didn't have to project
  that someone had a special ability to do it.

If only it didn't take a Christ walking by
  so we could touch the hem of his robe.

Joe Blow could walk by
  and we could touch the hem of his robe
  and be healed.

Do you realize what that could mean
  if you and I, if each of us
  had the freedom to know
  that we are a religious experience.

Not that we're having a religious experience.
But that we are a religious experience
  simply by the quality of our attention.

I suspect that most
of the conceptual frameworks
around various forms
of energy healing work

are mental defenses against the unknown
not realistic expressions of the actual
phenomena that's happening.

You have to come towards this Mystery
as best you can creating a frame of reference in
yourself that's not a defense, not a separation.

For me the frame of reference is
the expression of my love of the Mystery
and my love of the other.

You don't go to work
vainly thinking 'I'm a healer'
you go to work
gladly praying 'I'm a servant'.

And how can you call work
that which the intelligence of the Universe
ordains anyway.

If what we're doing
is making up something out of our heads
it won't have much life.

But what if what we're doing
is remembering the indwelling intelligence
and finding ways to reveal that to ourselves?

THE deepest possible relationship
I can have to you
whether in words or in silence
is a relationship of no intent
no desire to do anything to you
no understanding of what could be invoked here.

You see I don't know what you need.
I don't know what to do.
I'm just sitting here.

Now this is either disaster
   and the moment of failure
   or revelation
   if you will reciprocate
   and make this holy
   this is the door to a most profound relationship.

THE ultimate therapeutic technique

is to celebrate the presence of God

in the person of another.

Body Consciousness

STOP FOR A MOMENT and notice whereabouts in your body you live. Probably it's in your head at a point just about midway between your eyebrows.

That's where most of us live, most of the time. We don't inhabit much of the rest of our bodies unless they happen to be either hurting us or delighting us. Right?

Now put your hand on your stomach just below the belly button and really focus your attention on it. Rub your belly, make small circles. What's happened to your thinking whilst you're focusing on your body? Make a deliberate effort to worry while your attention is on your stomach. You can't do it can you?

Some of the most ecstatic, exquisite moments of our lives happen when we get out of our heads and into the cells, into the movement, into the sensation and the subtlety of our bodies.

Movement, singing, particular kinds of meditation, prayer, exercise and focusing on the breath can all help us to experience greater consciousness of our bodies. Occasionally we may even step beyond consciousness *of* the body into consciousness *as* the body. This is an integrated state of awareness perhaps only experienced before as an infant—though then it was without the gift of being conscious of our consciousness.

As soon as
you lose your body
when you're not here
you have no referent
for the distinction of things.

The flowers
and the sunrise
are going to be spectacular
when you're right here
inside yourself.

But when you're not right here
inside yourself
you don't perceive them
as spectacular at all.

Where is your attention resting?

If it's not in your body,
    you'll have no reference
    to anything energetic.

It has to be in your body.

Anything that matters is in your body.
Fear, joy, love.
Anything.

WHY go to the trouble of doing body consciousness work?

Do you think it's all that important if you're flexible? Do you think it's all that important if you can bend or show off because you can get better postures than your friends?

Why waste the time if that's what you're doing?

How can you have faith
   if you aren't present in your whole organism?
   If you split off into thinking
   how could you be deeply receptive to
   what you're feeling?

To engage our deep feeling, to engage our sensuality
   and discover a profoundly new relationship to
   sensuality; that's what bodywork is about.

When you've listened
   and come deeply into your body
   and then you sit
   you become quiet and you can hear.

And all of our relationships
   are rooted in how deeply we're listening.

THE body hasn't changed a whole lot.
It's the most fundamental. It comes
closest to the truth.

And those things which change the most easily
   —attitudes, beliefs, thoughts and feelings
   they're a little further from the truth.

When we witness the mystery
   of spontaneous remission or the
   radical awakening of the heart
   then we're really in territory
   that forces us to our knees in wonderment.

And we have to start asking
   some very new questions
   about what we are.

Come back into
the sense of organism.
Breathe.

When you lose consciousness
of your breath
there's nothing
that roots you in yourself.

Stay with the gentle consciousness
of your breath.

Let awareness and the breath
become friends.

Feel the friendship.

BREATHING is crucial!
Every single breath
It will be like your anchor

Your attention will expand
   and expand and expand
      from the center of the breathing.

After you've danced and sung,
   after life has lived you
   physically, deeply,
   when you touch someone
   it's electric.

And what we see then
   is that we're in the presence of God.

Do we really think that
what we're supposed to do
is use our thinking
to rise out of our feeling
and out of our bodies?

Consciousness
is about incarnating
deeper and deeper into feeling.

Into a feeling relationship
with the Infinite Self.

The addiction
the demand for thinking

will be in direct proportion

to the degree to which
the body itself is not allowed

the degree to which
the body is rejected or denied.

PEOPLE who are so ungrounded
they can't stay here
usually have
all kinds of allergies.

The poor body is trying
to get them back home.

Wᴇ all have the capacity to see
and understand a thing
before we really know it
in our bodies

and we all know things
within our own beings
and our own bodies,
that we have a difficult time
trying to express.

❦   *A human being is comprised of trillions of
cells, all somehow expressing a single relationship—You or
Me. The intelligence of such a symphony of relationship is
incomprehensible.*

*What we can easily describe, manipulate, change (and
make a business out of) is always further from the core of us.
And that which lives as the core is mystery, so difficult to give
voice to.*

WHEN subject and object
come close together
when I am totally absorbed in what I do
I access enormous energy.

When skiing skis me
  I access enormous energy
  when the dance dances me
  I access enormous energy
  when the song sings the singer
  an energy radiates from that song
  that can have a whole audience in tears.

For years now my work
  has been about creating experiences
  of this larger body.

You have to take the journey yourself.

You must meditate,
  waken the energies of the body.

Yoga will awaken it
  exercise, jogging, dancing, lovemaking,
  worship and prayer will awaken it.
Sweat lodge will awaken it.

Walking in nature will awaken it.
Sitting quietly will awaken it.

*And everything that awakens if turned into
"the path", "the way", "the truth", or a routine or formula
will deaden us once again.*

B<small>LISS</small>
is often the result of disembodying.

And stress
is often the result
of embodying.

Incarnational movement is stressful
disincarnational movement is blissful.

If you're not in your body
you're not truly autonomous.

But if you can sustain
this tension
between stress and bliss
that is your embodiment
and your enlightenment.

The more supple, alive, yet ordinary you are
the more you can partake of the universal energy
without being ripped
out of your body
out of your mind.

WHEN the body gets so relaxed
and the breathing so spacious
that the current of self-awareness
dissolves into the ocean of being
that's blissing out.

And we all love to bliss out.

Trouble is
    when you bliss out
    no one's home.

But one of the places we can grow the most
    is at the edge where self-awareness and the
    ocean of being meet.

That
    is a threshold to a vast, vast world.
    It's much bigger than
    the current of self-awareness
    but when you can stay with the two
    subtly touching each other
    there's a quality that's right here
    and it stays with the breathing
    and it's blissful
    as opposed to blissed out.

The Alchemy of Relatedness

THE word alchemy has its roots in antiquity. It traveled from Greece via Rome to Middle English and has lodged in our language ever since.

An alchemist was a scholar and adept whose life was dedicated to discovering alkanal, a mystical substance which was thought to act like a universal solvent dissolving base metals so they could be turned into gold.

In Richard's work, the word *alchemy* suggests the power inherent in our capacity for relationship to create subtle transformation within us. Conscious relationship acts as a solvent on the barriers in the psyche that prevent us from realizing the true gold of our human potential.

Relatedness is used broadly here, not confined to our primary love relationship, but extending to our relationship with ourselves, with life, with other beings, with mystery and with God.

CAN you feel that place inside of you
that's wanted approval
and acceptance and love

precisely because
you haven't found it in yourself.

When the love of yourself is deep
it no longer reaches outside
and requires it of someone else.

When you can say of your mother or father
I no longer need you to understand me
I no longer need your approval
I no longer need you to be safe.
My sense of myself is
between me and God now.

The relationship between me
and my parents or spouse or anyone
is really what has grown between me and God
me and my essence
me and my soul.

🕯 *To love yourself as it is used here is not narcis-
sism or egoistic self-involvement all of which rests on an
unconscious fear of nothingness. True self love is a radical
transformation in the root of our identity from the ego's fear
of being nothing, to the self's fundamental sense of connection.
This whole book is a description of this transformation.*

WHEN someone's opinion of you
pulls you away from
a sense of connection to yourself
that's suffering.

But when someone's opinion of you
negates you
but doesn't
pull you away from yourself
that's pain.

And pain we can bear.
Lots of pain.

Pain's not the problem.
It's finally getting grounded in ourselves
and not losing ourselves,

Not being afraid
to have our own experience
and finally stand
up in it.

CHILDREN who feel deeply safe in their bodies
are children who'll be able to
surrender their egos
and merge with the larger consciousness,
join with the evolutionary force
far more readily
than children who feel
terribly wounded and abandoned
deep down in their bodies.

The best investment
that we can possibly make
as a society
is in fostering our evolutionary potential.

The cumulative effect
of a few generations of deeply loved children
will be an unrecognizable world.

Wᴇ are called to each other
by a deep inner
song of recognition.

We sense the radiance
of each other's aliveness.

The door of the soul
into the timeless
that has been opened.

SOMETIMES you ask a question
as if you want intimacy
but the place you ask the question from
guarantees you won't get it.

Who is asking the question?
Does your question have its roots in unconscious desires:
wanting approval, wanting control, wanting understanding,
wanting security?

If moment by moment, you can feel and release these wants,
the space that remains is where intimacy happens.

IF a person doesn't have pride
and deep, deep self esteem
and they go hand in hand
they're not going to try
to be the living demonstration
of the magnificence of our world.

They're going to be careless
half hearted, poorly focused.

You can't do anything
worth doing
without pride.

And it's a razor's edge
between pride that obliges us
and arrogance that stunts us.

Avoiding relationship is about avoiding pain.

The limit of our faith
   is the amount of suffering we can bear
   or the amount of feeling we can accept
   before it becomes fear.

This growing expanse is the prayer that is each of us.

Ｈow do we know that we're living rightly?

What if we've never lived it wrong?
What if our sorrow and our pain
  and our rage and our fear
  and our distrust
  were just the heartbeat
  we haven't yet learned to listen to
  or the breath we haven't studied.

To explore them
  to inquire into them thoroughly
  that, to me, is being responsible.

Take a quiet space and ask yourself: How do I avoid relationship to myself? How do I avoid relationship to others? Then follow each answer back to the underlying feeling that you are protecting against. What you won't allow yourself to feel into and release past becomes the limit of your reality.

IF a person has a center
it will become everyone's center
and they won't give themselves away
to the anxiety of the new.

This is the transmission
of faith.

ALL expansion of consciousness
all spirituality must ground
in our humanity
in our capacity to love,
touch, communicate
and share together.

Enlightenment is becoming
more fully human.

THE real guru is the energy of our association.

If someone can let me be me
   and let themselves be themselves
   then a presence comes.

And that presence animates us
   that presence transforms us in ourselves
   changes our way of thinking about life
   and our feeling into life.

And that presence is the teacher.

Ultimately
intelligence is faith.

The only really intelligent relationship
   to anyone including ourselves
   is profound and utter trust
   in the vastness of us.

WHAT happens when we judge
is that we define ourselves
and usually it is a
poor definition.

IT takes tremendous maturity to meet life
    to meet all of life
    and not to make ourselves wrong in it
    to drink our individual cups of Gethsemane
    and not demean ourselves with self-pity.

And that's what makes us radiant.
It's not that we seek to suffer.
It's not that we seek to have pain.
The most difficult cup to drink
    is when we don't know
    where we're being self destructive
    or just being true to life.

We're navigating that kind of territory now
    as individuals and collectively.

We don't know whether
    we're going towards apocalypse
    or towards
    some quantum leap of consciousness.

I think where we are being required to go
    is to a deeper and more humble embrace of life
    and taking conscious responsibility
    for all our relationships.

Our egos want to be lights that shine happiness
but we're lights that shine everything.

And if we weren't lights that shine everything
the universe would be a very small
and shabby universe indeed
because it couldn't possibly
have given us the capacity for consciousness
and then said that's only going to be
the positive and pleasing
pole of consciousness.

You know I try to think to myself
how have I learned gradually over time
not to run away from my own experience
from the habit of identifying with my own experience.

For instance
    'Oh that's a pain', I'll change my position.
    'Oh that's sadness',
    I'd better do something else
    or that's because so and so
    said such and such to me.

And we're so convinced
    that we've explained
    why we've experienced
    what we've experienced.

But that's only one explanation
    and what we call a reasonable
    or rational explanation for sensation or feeling
    is not the only explanation
    and many times it's not the best explanation.

Because it's usually a Godless explanation
    it's usually the explanation of our ego
    that thinks it's God
    that lives in a closed world
    and thinks that everything is referent to itself.

WE enter into a relationship to grow, to change,
to heal, to transform, to be lifted, to understand
and these are good.

But this very intent is defining us
and that is a very familiar level.

We have been wanting to grow and understand
wanting to change and transform,
wanting to heal ourselves and others
wanting to serve.

We have been doing all those things
and we will continue to do all those things.

But right now in this moment
let us simply celebrate God.

Nothing more or less.
Just celebrate God.

W<small>HEN</small> we become vulnerable to a feeling that we
don't know what to do with, that's when we ask
deep questions about our lives.

And the beauty of it is that when you're anguishing
here on a summer night, someone's just going about her job
on a wintry day somewhere else on the planet.

The closedness of some of us
in our daytime ego drivenness
is balanced
by the vulnerability of others
in their night time trials.
We're not just living these things by ourselves.

And what we do to stop defending ourselves
against feeling and vulnerability gives everyone
everywhere the opportunity to live life
with a little more authenticity
and a little more mystery.

We can't keep living in this insulated littleness
protecting and figuring out *me* and wanting to
know about *me* in this very small way
that doesn't lead to God
that doesn't lead to the mystery
and the wonder of myself
to the terror of myself.

And our lives are pretty shallow without that.

If we truly understood
  where the Infinite starts
  and that the only possible relationship
  to the Infinite is faith

We'd put our bags down.

We'd put our bags down
  for life exactly as it is.

The yielding available to us right now
  isn't attained by knowing what we're doing
  but precisely because we don't know
  what we're doing and we act anyway.

We act with greater and greater vulnerability
  greater and greater unknowing,
  greater and greater uncertainty
  and it is rare indeed for someone
  to reach the point
  where they know
  that nothing in our relationship
  is as fundamentally real
  as the fact that I am God
  and you are God.

And the level of maturity
  required for that
  is enormous.

We are part of the one continuous
web of consciousness
and every time we step
a little closer to integrity
and aren't afraid to face feeling
it gets a little easier for everyone.

Every time we get
a little more authentic in ourselves
everyone finds it easier to be more authentic.

Iғ ours is a loving God.
  we live in a loving world

If ours is an angry God
  we live in a hostile world

This isn't a choice
  this is Realization.

The Awakening Soul

To TALK ABOUT The Awakening Soul, implies that the soul sleeps. What sleeps isn't the soul but our awareness of it in our lives. Life beckons us to awaken to our true nature.

A teaching story tells of a Zen disciple who goes to his master and asks that he be granted advancement to a higher level of being. He wishes to become enlightened.

"*Why don't you ask for a horse?*" says the master.

"*But I already have a horse!*" the disciple replies.

The master is silent.

How can we awaken to what we already are?

W<small>HEN</small> you engage, really say yes to truth
when you answer the call
anything that's not in harmony
with the deeper intelligence
goes to hell.

Anyplace where you're lying to yourself
anyplace where you've compromised
will be in your face within a year.

Ruthlessly. Absolutely ruthlessly.

What we've consecrated to
It will rework our circuitry
It will rework our relationships
It may utterly rework the circumstances of our life.

The same intelligence
that guides and holds this universe together
is emerging in our lives
and it won't let us lie to ourselves.

❦   *To become whole we have to make room for*
what we've hidden from, pushed away or denied as ourselves.
Psychologically, these disowned aspects are called the shadow,
but this term is deeply misunderstood. The shadow is not
merely negative character traits, it includes whole potentials
of beingness, dimensions of perception, awareness, energy
and life forces that needed to be repressed in early childhood
to create the bounded ego that is the basis of our sense of
separate self.

THE beauty of the awakening energy
is that it humiliates us.

You don't become larger and grander on your terms
you awaken and you get burned
you get humbled
you get scared to death
you tremble in your bed at night.

Have you noticed this enormous sadness
this deep, deep burning feeling
in the heart,
this kind of grief
that's there day in and day out
with no apparent reason at all?

Not that happiness isn't possible eventually
but we don't understand this mourning
this dying of the old self.

There's something about mourning
that makes us more able to be
conductive of life.

The Sufis speak of this as
the 'Broken Heart of God'.

❧   *And we do not merely integrate these repressed
dimensions by imagining we can add them on to our existing
sense of self. We are called to sensations, feelings, energies
we cannot understand. We may feel we're dying or going
mad, but this is just the ego's interpretation. Allowing this
process deeply, we emerge more whole and authentic than
ever before. Welcome to transformation.*

THE people who speak about true enlightenment
talk about a sudden, complete and total realization.

They say it is never a gradual process.
    It's a total and complete change of heart
    change of being, change of mind
    a radical and profound
    fundamental transformation.

I say absolutely that's true,
    all at once, "in a moment, in a twinkling of the eye".

But enlightenment in that sense
    remains unborn, unexpressed and has no meaning
    until it becomes relationship.

Enlightenment in the world is a seasoning process
    a ripening process
    you engage and live
    and listen and receive
    and are transformed and changed
    by the relationship with the other.

*Being embodied is not an accident, not a mistake.
Enlightenment is not escape from the limitations of the body,
but an ever deepening recognition and acceptance of our
humanness.*

WE become radiant
when we stand in that center place
within the triangle
of me
my neighbor
and God.

We're fearful
when we forget God
and we're just self-involved.

We're unauthentic
when we deny ourselves
and we're just in relationship to the other.

And we're unconcious when we forget ourselves, the other
and we're just entranced with God.

🌿   *When we "remember" ourselves there is no
distinction between self, other and God.*

ENLIGHTENMENT
is not an individual event.

Each of us
is a piece of this awakening entity.

No state of enlightenment is finished.
There's still an infinity
playing there somewhere
that could carry the enlightened person
anywhere.

Awakening is not a private gift, not a personal reward for our spiritual efforts. Awakening obliges us to an ever greater honoring of everyone and everything else. In this is the joy of awakening.

ANYTHING that unconsciously seduces us
to create self-identity
is antithetical
to awakening to this larger energy
and inevitably brings us suffering.

On the other hand
if we don't have strong ego-definition
we can't sustain
a meaningful collaboration
and co-creation with that larger energy.

We just get blown in the breeze of it.

*Healthy ego-definition comes from actively and
responsibly engaging life. And this means living out careers,
roles and all the daily responsibilities. But when we confuse
our real nature with the identities we attribute to our jobs or
for that matter to any ideas, feelings or moods, we have lost
contact with our Self and cannot draw energy from the larger
universe of which we are an integral part.*

Wᴇ bow our heads
　　and we turn away from life
　　and we say
　　whoops that's leading me
　　where I don't want to go.

We cannot really see what may come
　　if we live into something
　　in a way we've never lived before.

The mind says
　　Don't do that.
　　Go this way.
　　Here you can have what you can understand.

But something deeper often drives us
　　something deeper
　　whose fruit we cannot anticipate.

WE have this crazy idea that
life is supposed to reward us
and make us happy.

Relationships are supposed to make us happy.
Family is supposed to make us happy.
Therapy is supposed to make us happy.
Our spiritual work—that's the ultimate fix.

But what if it's not?
What if the Universe didn't create us
to make itself happy?

Happiness comes from being a part of Life, a part of the Universe. We do not exist as absolute separate entities. Trying to make what does not exist happy is futile.

IF we gain deep insight into life
and into ourselves
we find ourselves at times
deeply ashamed.

I don't mean just
a virulent judgementalness.
I mean there is something
we perceive about ourselves
that is such a profound wound
that it brings us to our knees.

What will it take for us to realize
the privilege of finally recognizing
what is called our life
and submitting to it?

THE Awakener?

You and I
we are the awakeners
of each other.

Awakening is a process
of infinite potential
and great ambiguity,
of dying and rebirth,
of meeting ourselves
in all the chaos of being.

THE problems
that are in our consciousness
problems of our capacity for intimacy
are really the worms
eating at our egos, painfully exposing the illusion
of separateness.

I had a direct experience
   of merging with everything
   of being at one with everything
   as much as I can talk about it
   of being at one with Existence.

I can say in truth
   that I know the state
   of I and the Father are One.
Not conceptually
Cellularly.

And you want to know something?
   So what!

It changed me physically.
It changed me psychically.
There was kundalini
   and there was this
   and there was that.

But it didn't prepare me for loving.
It didn't prepare me for divorce.
It didn't prepare me for kids.
It didn't prepare me for housework.

The real wonderment of life is being
   simply human.

If we're truly in a Nirvanic state
we're no longer evolving
so we have to soil ourselves once again
get down to the muck of life
and get involved
in a new dimension of complexity.

Nirvana works as long as
a great deal of life is excluded.
As soon as more of life is taken in
you can't be in Nirvana.

However if you've been in Nirvana
you'll trust bringing more of life in
you won't say 'no' to more of that complexity.

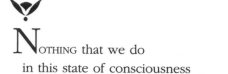

NOTHING that we do
in this state of consciousness
that we call being a human being

can assure us, can guarantee us
of Realization or Awakening.

We have to be humbled in this truth
and live with this wound
that we can't get there
through our own efforts

and

everything's possible in God.

Fundamental transformation is the manifestation of Grace and cannot be attained by ego-directed efforts because the ego itself, in the sense of a sovereign self-existent personage, is the basic illusion we must relax. But this should not be interpreted to mean that work on oneself is wasted effort. Skillful spiritual practice prepares us to maximize this Grace should it come and profoundly enriches our humanity.

WHEN you look out
at the universe, you might say
If this is not a loving universe
if there isn't integrity in this universe
then of course I'd better control things
I'd better fix me, move me in the right direction.

But if this is truly a loving universe
then what I'll do is I'll feel my pain
I'll truly see my dishonesty
I'll recognize my withholding
of intimacy in relationship.

I will be there.

And now I'm standing in front of this vastness
and I don't know how to
hold myself in the sensation of knowing
so the ego wants to use habitual patterns to sedate
and deaden
But I don't. I won't.

I wasn't given this taste of God to feel good
I wasn't given this love to be made happy or safe
I was given it to help me mirror to myself
what I am and what is.

And I don't want to be sedated.
If this relationship ends
it won't be because I close down or
split off from feeling.

IF we keep learning from our lives
we begin to see
that we can afford to have faith.

We don't have to try so hard.
We need to remind ourselves
who we really are
and we have to keep asking

"Am I reminding myself
because I'm really afraid
and I want to be the good child?"

"Or am I reminding myself
because the universe has been instructing me
about its magnificence
and I know I'm part of it?"

That's the razor's edge.

THE journey of faith comes
because we've met
feeling states inside of us
that we thought would overwhelm us
but we don't get overwhelmed
we get changed.

We recognize the intelligence
of that something inside of us
that tells us our story
with ruthless honesty.

It will tell us what we don't want to see
if that's what we need to see
and it will tell us we don't know how to see
when it's time for us to see.

Iɴ the journey of the soul
   the emptiness, the nothingness
   that we meet
   isn't really nothingness.

It's just the absence of the old intensity
   and your soul doesn't yet trust
   that you're going to plant seeds there.

But when it trusts that you'll plant seeds there
   things will grow in that soil
   that you call nothingness.

Things will grow there
   that can grow nowhere else.
   You see, in that nothingness
   relationship begins to take place
   in the domain of faith
   and faith is an extremely subtle thing.

Real faith is something hard won
   by setting aside the defensive contraction
   and the addiction to intensity
   and waiting nakedly...

When you dissolve that contraction,
   the basis for a self destructive relationship to life
   just disappears.

I F we can use the intelligence
of this awakening energy
to come to the root of our suffering
then we can also use it to meet
the fierce enigmas of interpersonal relationships.

*What do we really fear in our relationships?
Feeling. What we are unwilling to feel or believe ourselves
unable to feel defines the limits of our willingness to be honest,
to speak our truth without rancor, to be open-hearted and
loving. But who is afraid? Who is this special one, this separate
one, this important one? Relationships are great mirrors.*

Y OU have to do what is your gift,
what is your destiny.

No one can tell you what to do
and how to do it.

Information

For information on conferences, books, audio and video cassettes by Richard Moss, please contact the addresses and telephone numbers listed below:

U.S.A.
Richard Moss Seminars, P.O. Box 2147,
Oakhurst, CA (California), 93644. U.S.A.
Telephone: (559) 642-4090 Fax: (559) 642-4092
E-mail: miracle2@sierratel.com

ARGENTINA/URUGUAY
Cintia Posa
Carabelas 241 7 Piso
1009 Buenos Aires
Telephone: (541) 394-0543 Fax: (541) 394-0635

AUSTRALIA
The Vine and the Branches
27 Bonds Rd, Lower Plenty,
Melbourne, Victoria 3093
Telephone: (613) 4398248

Gill Goater
P.O. Box 1923,
Port Macquarie, 2444
Telephone: (065) 810074

FRANCE

Marie-Laure Fleury,
1 bis, rue du covent
34770 Gigean
Telephone: (01) 33-46-7786227   Fax: (01) 33-46-7787953

DENMARK

Svend Trier
Quantum Seminars
Emdrup Huse 27
DK-2100 Copenhagen
Telephone: 45-3929-0336

Sources

Cassette Tapes
  Journey of Unknowing (1984)
  Radiant Aliveness (1984)
  The Yoga of the New (1985)
  The Wound of Grace (1988)
  Bringing it all back home (1993)
  Integration(1993)
  Meditation(1993)

Conference Tapes
  Foundational Conference, Lone Pine, CA 1989
  Next Step Two Bend, Oregon, 1990,
  Melbourne, Australia, 1992, 1993, 1994, 1995

Lecture Tapes
  Sydney, Australia, 1992, 1993
  Melbourne, Australia, 1992, 1993

Mentor Conferences
  Mentor IV, U.S.A., 1994-1996

About the Author

Richard Moss received his Doctorate of Medicine in 1972, but after a few years of general practice a life-changing realization led him to his true calling: the exploration of spiritual awakening and its integration in daily life. For more than twenty years Dr. Moss has been helping people all over the world to touch their deeper essence and thus transform their lives. He lives with his wife in the foothills of the California High Sierras and has three grown stepchildren.

He is the author of five books that have been translated into five languages and speak with clarity and insight about the grace and obligation of this pivotal time in human evolution.

Acknowledgments

I would like to thank Gill Goater for conceiving the idea for this book and for the labor of love that brought it into being.
Thank you to Philip and Manuela Dunn for their help in making it a beautiful book.
Thanks to Roy Carlisle for his suggestions which added immeasurably to the book.
My special gratitude, as always, goes to my wife Ariel. She is in every meaningful sense a co-author of my work.